MOVING HOUSE

Theophilus Kwek is a writer, editor and translator based in Singapore. Two of his previous collections of poetry were shortlisted for the Singapore Literature Prize, while his pamphlet, *The First Five Storms*, won the inaugural New Poets' Prize in 2016. Other awards include the Jane Martin Poetry Prize, the Berfrois Poetry Prize, and the Stephen Spender Prize for poetry in translation. A former President of the Oxford University Poetry Society, he now serves as co-editor of *Oxford Poetry* and *The Kindling*, and has also edited several volumes of Singaporean writing. His poems, essays and translations have been published in *The Guardian*, *Times Literary Supplement*, *The Irish Examiner*, and the *Mekong Review*.

THEOPHILUS KWEK

Moving House

CARCANET

First published in Great Britain in 2020 by
Carcanet
Alliance House, 30 Cross Street
Manchester M2 7AQ
www.carcanet.co.uk

A CIP catalogue record for this book is
available from the British Library.

ISBN 978 1 78410 963 9

Book design by Andrew Latimer
Printed in Great Britain by SRP Ltd, Exeter, Devon

The publisher acknowledges financial
assistance from Arts Council England.

*For those who build our houses
and those who believe in keeping them open*

WITNESS

It was mid-morning. The body flipped,
came to rest face-down on tarmac.
Unaware, the rider went some distance
then, noticing something was amiss,
stopped, dismounted, ran back to where
a gathering clutch of men knelt and stood.
She was already gone. And so were we,
drawn on by the bus's trajectory
toward our stops, unseeing, unseen
except in one last receding frame.
Steep death. The mind trips at the shock,
chafes at conversation, replays the scene
till the point at which all fall unplanned –
what then? Imagining gains no ground,

is caught in a morning's too usual arc.
Hard pavement receives the pedestrian
in step as in flight, accounts to no-one
for what forces in our different lives
plot with foreign accuracy
lines of habit and desire, and bear us
away from accidents. Far behind now,
this leaving leaves its quiet mark. Parents,
asked by children about their days,
find fewer answers, tell only truths
and, passing afterwards, see in the place
of yesterday's routine a rupture
in our time, where past and present
futures meet, stop short. A living fault.

PROGNOSIS

The knowledge settles at the bottom of your glass.
What's left clarifies, divides the light. Clean white,
which crosses the air unscathed, and this – water's

half-true cataract. In its arc the table's dry laminate
turns gold-dappled, warm, even tiles rise up to dance.
Like a prism it drowns the ward in colour, albeit

of one tan shade. How is it that outside bears no trace?
A vaulted sky hovers as if on steel beams to clothe
a station hall. Cars idle at the roundabout, nurses

stride with great purpose from block to block
yet nothing resembles this: how here the day transforms
and slows, its swollen alchemy. Bedside, your clock

mocks us both, pilfering with gloved hands from
every hour, while time, stealing through your un-
finished cup, lays itself down, the sun's bright psalm.

Before this dull image in the blood's darkroom,
you too pursued your tricks of the lens, drove so often
from one station to another, in some unknown realm

with your camera to mark the breaking of night or dawn.
I could not see then, why a moment's flux
should arrest your gaze, or why with determination

you'd try and snare each one for eternity. Now I look
on as the rays unspool across your desk and feet, listen
for coughs, how your engine lingers with lifted clutch,

and gather up the spent threads from where I stand.
It falls on my fingers too, this ravelling light.
I wish I could glean it with more than hands.

CHINESE WHISPERS

'It always turns out that much is salvageable.'
       — John Ashbery (1927–2017)

Have you heard   how we light up the houses
     so they last forever, pyres of cardboard and joss
with laughter in the windows, late guests
     dressed in their best clothes for a midnight ball
and all the old flames still dancing, long past
     the hour?   We cannot count the pairs
(stacks of legal tender for a bank above,
     a paper chariot sent to speed the road ahead,
shoes without soles: what use are they
     to ghosts?...) each one tossed across the chasm
becoming its better, each translated without
     loss, salient as prayer   *I was a phantom
for a day,* you said and we believed you then,
     set our own spells to paper like fire so they
would catch, would work with some new
     and unheard-of efficacy   or even travel
whole continents in a night as yours could, held
     aloft   by the heat of their own significance,
only to be visible a while from this world, from
     ours, but also from yours   or whichever you
resolved to inhabit then   or (having gone
     yourself now where we cannot understand) might
so alight   or ever will   and without end.

MY GRANDFATHER VISITS PYONGYANG

Too late, we find among his photographs
a kingdom mostly dreamed of,

its absurd architecture where
he alighted some time in October.

Frame after frame resists comparison.
There isn't a place we've seen

that stands as still, or with the same intent
raises its glass towards heaven,

all normalcy locked within a sound
these pictures don't contain – a pitch rung

in the earth's confines, too low
for human hearing. Friends tell us to allow

ourselves the time it takes
to grieve, or whatever brings us back

to last year's long continuum,
but something stays the eye. How in some

perspectives he's already gone,
gone from the boulevards where wide-crowned

trees fill up the viewfinder,
and men and women in work clothes hover

outside our field of vision. He's
somewhere else entirely, now close,

now looking in, the disappearance
nothing more than a trick of the lens,

though we fall for it again and again.
How like him, we think,

then catch ourselves. The leaves turn
on their own impulse in our hands.

REQUIEM

You met us again in the outer room.
White bone in miniature, glazed earth
parting the skull's cracked continents.

With love's red cloth covering the bowl,
we lined up one by one to send you home.
A pair of hands took each broken part

and joined it with the others in the pile
so the pieces belonged as they were laid,
tibia, sternum, pelvis, patella

nook to nook, against the plain design.
In cupped fingers we scooped the fire-
tempered sand, a cloud of chalk

over the precious hill. You said nothing,
content that we should have our ways of loss,
our sifted, falling silences, the plunge

of numbed hands under frigid water.
Teach me now to love, at their frayed edges
the left-behind, their washed and ashen fingers.

THE GAMBLE

'Oh-yah-pay-yah-sohm', lit. 'black-and-white-and-count': a
system for drawing lots, where all players display their palms
at the same time, either facing up or down; a children's game.

Believe me when I say it meant everything
not to be caught with your palm open,
pearl-white and marking you out among
sunned knuckles, wrists wrapped in veins,
nails rich and streaked with too much earth.

One wrong move could cost an afternoon,
seeing as there was no deliverance
from being chosen by your own hand
as *fire*, *hunter*, damned to the far-fetched chance
that your quarry, set free at a touch

might run out of steam, or in a moment's
distraction deliver an unlucky ally.
And so all our longer hours were spent
in fruitless pursuit, until finally
what began to dawn as a kind of truth –

even then – became inescapable.
The empty hand, the curse of the chase, fear
driving through the field of broken hurdles,
a parched track, grass beaten under...
Too close, the cut of childhood's metaphors

for shorter days in taller houses,
far safer to keep the children indoors
than have them learn, by trial if not error
how after each round, our hands' imperfect work
was forgiven by their turning over.

MAGDALENE

For days afterwards late spring took its course.
A north wind came through the window-slats
and plovers returned to walk on water.
In the shorter shadows the city's groves
filled out with leaves, promised black olives
as clouds wept and bowed over the temple.
We broke bread on the roof. Said fumbling prayers
to keep the hours, returned to usual squares,
gathered each evening in our knit circles.
It was all we could do to live, despite
the wanting the waiting or the altered light
of that once-opened sky, blue as a miracle.
In time, we grew acquainted with the weight
of wonder; thought less of the mystery of things,
thought them more believable. Some went back
to Galilee. Others made for other seas,
nets and fresh tackle. I watched them leave,
then stood alone in the tug of wild hyssop
at the city's sleeve, strong as love or the facts
of being known: brief night. The lightness of stone.

THE DANCE
for Grandmother (1940 – 2017)

This year, he says, *there will be no dance.* [1] Better to let the old house rest,

its spirits cool, settle themselves as the earth sleeps fallow. We come

forward with cupped hands, and as the custom is, leave store-bought shoes

> [1. The third day they'd arrive, wrapped in beating colours,
>   with their mandarins, excuses for tardiness, drums
>   to wake a neighbourhood. Always a day of gladness,
>   a day for noise, so no-one held it against them;
>   everybody knew they'd stop at grandma's gates,
>   everyone said they weren't watching but they were.
> *The biggest lion in Limau Purut, once a year only,*
>   *come, come. Eh you, why you want to stay inside?*]

and greetings by the door; make tea, small talk. Set ourselves at home. For

the first time in years [2] I am here, home for the other New Year, the first

time also she will not join us at the table. Big Uncle takes her place, and as

[2. Close enough, but we'd still drive Sunday evenings
            to the house for dinner, a quiet living-room affair
            with the TV on, the nights long gone
            when all of us cousins could squeeze on the swing
            without embarrassment. Half the time we'd find her
            out in front, wrist-deep, pulling up the bad grass
    from the porch, *my own piece of the earth* she'd say,
            and with the cold steel of garden scissors close by.]

the fragrant noodles are served, we fall into our usual conversation. I try

to remember the scene: the men muscling through the open door, a kind

of fierce purpose in their gold finery, [3] even the wild leaps, the daring falls

[3. Only much later that I knew, holding her bright jacket
            round her shoulders so it wouldn't slip, how it was
            she'd come to plant herself where she stood, to build
            the house (and all it held) around her, out of nothing,
            out of the earth itself, by her knuckles, by her own arms,
            her bad knee that made her give up on the garden.
    It was her first time visiting, in the cold climate;
            and this new orange jacket *a gift from your father*.]

of the dance. Do I know what it means, I wonder, to be as they are, so intent

on their work of blessing? *Maybe next year,* father laughs, which brings me

back to the table, but then I hear the beats outside, know they're already here.

DEAD MAN'S SAVINGS WON'T GO TO WIFE

'Ms Diao … claimed to love Mr Soon and to meet him for dinner
about once a week, but could not say why she loved him.'
— *The Straits Times*, 8 September 2016

How could I explain? *Your first glance*
was that of an old lover's. All guilt,
no charm. As I washed the breakfast things
you struggled with your shirt, belt,

looked away when I knelt
to lace your shoes. Those mornings
turned out to be my favourite –
us two in the park downstairs,

your arm on mine as joggers passed,
wings touching as we flew. Months
wore on. You ate little, spoke less,
but still I knew you'd *give a thousand coins*

for my smile, the way you'd sit
by the door waiting, or press a little extra
into my palm as I went to market
for threadfin or garoupa,

something for myself. For you this
was enough, an extravagance, nearly,
of joy. And I? *I loved the house*
and the crows that nested there,

the missed appointments, separate beds,
how you always left the radio on.
In the end, they said,
you gave no last instructions,

so it wasn't clear my claim was genuine.
That, I tried not to mind.
I wish you'd told them how much this would mean.
One who knows my voice is hard to find.

* *Italics denote loose translations of Chinese idioms for love:*
一见如故, 比翼双飞, 千金买笑, 爱屋及乌, 知音难觅.

BLUE

Years later, I saw in the Ashmolean
precious plates, fine porcelain

of the best handiwork, that stood
down the aisle on the first floor

in their blue cases. Some of them by then
I already knew by heart, having gone

to school in the refurbished building
where we painted, one year, a semblance

of a low Victorian house that sat out of reach
as our bus-route narrowed to a bridge.

Others I had never seen, but were the twins
of a bright, winding city where I spent

hours salvaged from school and home
with my own widening strides marking time,

close likenesses copied onto each gleaming
dish from Calcutta and Penang.

Behind Grandmother's house there was once
a factory where, in her motley tongue,

she told me they used to blow blue glass
for windowpanes, wine-bottles, flasks.

I pressed my hands to the cabinet
full of china, and dreamt that I could touch

the tea services, with their beautiful necks
too thin, too tall for proper use.

HUANG XUEYING MEETS HER MOTHER IN THE UNDERWORLD

In 2006, the Thai government granted citizenship to remaining members of the Malayan Communist Party, allowing them to return to Malaysia as visitors. They had lived in the jungle for fifty years.

When I came back, they said you'd gone
to the temple with a whole month's savings

tucked in a sleeve, your best skirt, a sack
of mangoes to charm the medium. One look

beneath the surface, eyes blazing, and she
had picked out one who looked like me. *She's*

dead, she said. You stood – *what nonsense!* –
spat on the floor, swept toward the house

with the children in tow, but two weeks later
there you were again with a prayer

Fourth Uncle had copied out in large writing.
For years after, you came at each new moon

with some bruised fruit, rice packed in a leaf;
one time, even, a small portion of lamb, left

over from great-grandfather's visit. In time
you stopped calling, leaving not a soul at home

as I found, climbing the old wooden stair; no
coming or going, not like we were used to

in those days, before we knew hunger or worth,
or this still seeking, this other life.

THE PASSENGER

'After the tsunami, taxi drivers reported picking up ghost passengers who asked to be brought to their destination and then disappeared, leaving their fare unpaid.'
— *Inquisitor*, 4 February 2016

This, then, is the afterlife. A bend, a
shout, a breath of diesel, morning's murmur

staining the kerb a shade of persimmons.
A solitary confinement. No-one

else in line, birds passing like vehicles
and this way from Sendai, Charon's vessel

an old Corolla pulling up close. In
our stories, the dead follow the whirlwind

of a river's course underground, until
it comes up for air. The earth is a bell

that trembles only with water's voice
or when struck with an unnatural force,

as when Izanagi drew a fire from
his whalebone comb, and saw in the loam

his beloved, Izanami, asleep
at the foot of the well. How the god wept,

afraid! Then turned, and, bashful of his fear,
sealed death's throat with a stone. So here we are

without refuge. Out from the silent town
to the highway's shoulder, fog-lights, the sound

of brakes, front tyres arresting earth. Chassis,
an open window. Lock, both doors. Release.

WESTMINSTER

I.

Broken light, high water. Here and elsewhere
the cold thought of something beyond belief
settling into movement – an unstoppable design –
lodges in the throat, will not be sung.
We fall on words made for other means:
Visibility, four miles. More clouds than sun.

II.

Within days, it seems, this injury
will join the rim of that other, deeper cut
over which no scar can form. Unclean, unshut.
As yet it gapes distinct: flesh wound, a loss
without name and yet no easier
to reckon, its surface so bare of facts
except the act of loss itself, no choice
or distance, no motive, no face, no legend,
(a mere expanse which holds the skin apart)
no way to map the way to map a way.

III.

Lines open for interchange. The earth trembles,
holds fast this steel heart, its brave circulation,
every safe passage a jubilee. Who are they
whose paths must cross at our deepest station?

IV.

Already, without doubt, we have begun to fear
and fear the upshot of fear, the lightning and the storm.
But darkness now, which passes for calm.
                                        A prayer:

V.

For each morning that takes place unawares.
The still scalding shower. The flight of stairs.

OCCURRENCE

Thames Valley Police, No. 43150331197

6.35 p.m. on 23rd November, 2015: the victim was struck on the face
with a metal rod by men in an unidentified car, on Oriel Square,
breaking his glasses. No assailant could be traced.

Nothing much then, now nearly unseen –
a cut beneath the eye. A bruise, fading
to skin, frown and furrow, fine print. How

soon the body grieves, forgives how easily
it gives. Already these marks are marks
of other things. Sleepless lines that mar

an early frost. Fields turned for planting,
sandstone shorn against the river's brink.
A fishhook's incline, the doubling pitch

of flight like a whaler's reckoning. In
the hollow of a bridge the water leaves
no scar, only trembling. A sound gone

as if from a whipped bowstring, between
where the arrow flies and, at each end,
thread spliced so as to pucker wood: the eyes.

MONOLOGUES FOR *NOH* MASKS

Pitt-Rivers Museum, Oxford

i. A god who has taken the form of an old man

Early November a narrow seam unzips,
fills up with rain. The whole earth is untuned.
In the water's timbre is both pain and sleep.
Take my word: these are the things I knew.

ii. A young man, who has not yet adopted the conventions worn by older men

Father tells us it is no surprise, a bad year.
Harvests come and go. By next winter we'll have made back
our loss, replenished the stores, turned the ship around.
I don't ask why I've seen him count up our stock,
or, in the stables long after the men have gone,
brush his favourite horse from head to hoof,
run gloved hands through her hair as if to comfort both.
Without her there is no way he can draw the plough,
turn our old mill, take the grain to market,
or ride home over the road from a day in the fields
and tell us it is no surprise, harvests come and go.

iii. An ageing woman who cannot enter the next life

Easier to say *the time wasn't right.* Or,
I did what I could, and though whatever

you did was nothing, is nothing, these
are not lies. In time you become used

to the charge (which is the power to shock)
that you have less to own up to, in fact,

than you thought. Less, even, than nothing.
Apart from this there is no reckoning.

iv. The ghost of a man in the world of both the living and the dead

Touch me to your temple. I've heard it said
this is how it feels to be afraid.

24.6.16

*Red kites, native to Turkey, Morocco, and parts of Europe, were
declared 'vermin' by the English crown and hunted nearly to
extinction. They were successfully reintroduced to the UK in 1989.*

No red kites over the field this morning.
However hard I looked, I could not find

a single cresting pair, their high crosses
invisible – as if unpitched from the grass.

No dry swoop, no sounding. No clatter from
morning's fed sparrows rising in alarm,

no hare's carcass eaten behind our wall,
nothing astir. No courting on the fell

in curious patterns, no stumbling display
of swift shadows bending above the Wye.

No haunt. No song. Only the heaven's blue
graceless fire, and then as a ghost pursued

across a moor, the hunting-horn's burly
cry
                    crucify, crucify, crucify.

STRANGERS DROWNING

'[We learned] that a Singapore navy patrol boat had intercepted a
sinking refugee boat but left them to drown [...] The government later
blamed the young conscript officer in command of the boat.'
— Resettlement officer; Canadian High Commission, 1979

Now what returns is this: the dread
of Tuesday mornings at the neighbourhood pool,

zipped to the throat in a new suit tightening
with the slow plunge of the poolside stair

and you, cajoled, abashed, but pushed
nonetheless to a certain fate, alive

as the water's vice rises past knees
chest shoulders to seal around

your eyes, throw the world off-whack. Only
eleven, and already willing to believe

in nothing but the woman who stands
on dry land, with a towel and thermos yelling

your name, her voice a lost song, the prayer
your mouth mouths. For air. For air.

*

Two people are drowning: your aged mother
and a child you have never seen. There
is room in the boat for one, no questions.
Who will you rescue? The philosopher's
features are kind, inscrutable. Somewhere
a window closes. Another opens.

*

Last one to put your head underwater, still
kicking the wet ledge, you swallow

as the guard kneels to prise your fingers off.
How you envy the others! Their luck

and their quick beauty, oh what it would mean
not to have the hour undone

by a dream of drowning! But envy will not
loose your welded grip. Hauled stiff-limbed

to life each week, the wall's brute hold
leaves your fingers cut. You show them off

at school to those for whom the dread
is still too much. *How brave*, they are full

of praise. *How clever!* Your feet feel
again the rough tiles beneath them.

*

Now think again: this time there is only
the child. Speck in the eye, small infinity,
defying the curved sea. There is no choice.
We must save her, yes? The philosopher asks
with a gleam. What then to hear of the same
but multiplied, at a distance, and unnamed?

*

Woken with twice the urgency, the men
fall quickly into routine, muster

where the gunboats, tarred and polished,
have long been waiting. With deft ease they

fill their stations, you among them
chosen for your sharp eye to man the watch,

knowing only to impress and not knowing
better. So tell no-one what you have seen –

not the raft, misshapen, that doggedly
comes into view – but your own men

ordered to stand to and promptly riven,
not daring to move or to believe. Some

still shy of nineteen. Their faces like
the distant faces are wet as the sea.

*

Death knows no distance, so why should we?
The philosopher has no answer
but pushes on; oblivious, accustomed maybe
to this unease. And what if the child were
just slightly older, a young man, who in
another life might keep the watch, unmoving?

*

Weeks later you are in the papers, you
and your crew *scouring the sea*

to save lives, and though the photograph
is nondescript, showing faces

you only faintly recognize, everyone
wants to know *were you scared, did they*

try anything, how many bad guys
were among them? Within days you have

a story prepared; in it the men, fearful
at first, pull off a brave rescue,

and you – you find yourself saying – are
looking on, proud. There must be

truth in this, it comes so naturally.
In time even you will forget this story.

*

Time's passage is a frugal thing. It keeps
its own hours, stations; shortens distances,
discards much else. The philosopher
leans back into his seat as he says this
and settles into silence, or even sleep.
You stand quietly and open the door.

*

*Somewhere in the Indian Ocean are boats
of people,* the radio says, *who will never*

*be rescued. Somewhere there are children,
mothers too,* their fathers having long

undone themselves to lessen
the water's pull on what is in any

case a graceless vessel. Flow, drag.
There must be other words for what happens

but these are yours, and are sufficient.
Somewhere whole villages the radio goes

on, or would go on, but is suddenly tuned
to music, something from the seventies.

His eyes, in the mirror, apologize.
This is a death you can both believe in.

THE WEEK IT HAPPENS

for 3rd Sergeant Gavin Chan, killed in peacetime training

this is how we build a wall   around a name
the week it happens   we are told   to speak
of the dead is   to speak ill   that there is no
room   for speculation or idle talk   he says
only facts have a place   and even so we will
not say anything   not post on Facebook   or
Twitter   there is a quiet in the room   some
are checking their phones   maybe they have
said something   without thinking that might
be taken as speculation maybe   they are just
on Instagram   this is   he continues   this is
to spare a thought   for the family of the boy
he corrects himself   man   he means young
man   but there is a pause   nobody hears it
as if he loses his voice   immediately after he
says boy   the word   it hangs   in his throat
sounding   like it has been caught   trying to
escape   a careful fence   a tall one   raised
precisely to stop this from happening   these
are the facts   as they take place   an order
of events   the boy   for let us call him that
is in command   of an armoured vehicle   a
tank   he is guiding it   as it travels through
difficult terrain   it falls on its side   and he
is found unconscious   it happens   quickly
in situations like this   the auditorium is very
quiet   we have been asked   to sit with our
backs straight   nobody breathes so it's hard
to say   what anyone   *thinks*   but here we
are   boys   young men   and scared of dying

WHAT IT'S LIKE

How do I tell you now about the way
they placed it in his hands, a baby's weight,
just as tenderly pulled his shoulders back
to take the heave and coil, every fresh blow
leaving him sore, the sour echo of *this
is how you kill a man?*

     *It takes a man
to do that for his country*, they said, and there
in the wet scrape it seemed almost true,
knowing a body's length of new earth lay
upturned, packed tight to rest his barrel on,
not daring to move, legs and torso stained
with an afternoon's digging, as ten a time
slipped away to practice advancing
from point to point, or picking up the dead,
the whole earth shattering beneath them.
Don't be scared,

     these aren't even live.
He learned to play dead, always the lightest
in the group, the one his friends would plan
to evacuate, arms crossed over one
another's to stabilize the casualty, last man
claiming his rifle where it fell *so we don't
give the rascals anything.*

     *If you're lucky,
he's still breathing* (and always, the refrain)
if not, don't move him.

     It's hard to tell
the truth of it – even half, he thinks – but these
are the things he knew, or maybe knows now,
or wishes he did, is what I'm saying.

THE FALL

for Private Dave Lee Han Xuan, killed in peacetime training

Marching before dawn. Heat rises in haggard lines
as the earth, the colour of ash, moves to hold us.

    On the road, a cloud. The colour of ash, felled cloud,
    an immaculate thing. The earth moves. A breath.

You see it first. Distant, then suddenly here. A breath:
the body of a bird, small felled thing, cloud of ash.

    Our two lines part. The body of a bird, it moves us,
    even in death. Distant, suddenly seen. A thing of breath.

Something about death. We know our parts, lines,
move without falling. Distance, heat, cloud, ash –

    but no, rituals are for later. First, you see it. Dawn colour,
    ragged heat, and what is earth becoming breath –

fallen: still immaculate. Cloud body, cloud breath.
Dawn as a line of flight. Not earth. Nor death,

    the raggedness of it. Suddenly your own small heat
    becomes ash, falls as cloud. Wetting the earth,

immaculate as dawn, night's breath. The road
marches on, unmoved by this heat, this death,

    the suddenness of it. Hold this: the small body
    of a bird, of ash. For all that is seen rises as breath.

H.

Haggai of Oxford, a Christian Deacon and student of Hebrew,
was burnt alive in 1222 after embracing the Jewish faith 'for
the love of a Jewess'.
— The Dunstable Annals

The sum of his possessions when
we took him: mortar, pestle. An

inkwell, dry. Fine dye, coins to weigh
leaves of grammar, a pillow for

the wrist. Robes, bound in crisp paper.
Where he towelled his feet after

rain, a stool, chiselled to a squat.
Outside the door a low stair led

under the alley where they mourned
their lost seamstress and her husband

to a musty basement, and here
we found last year's olives in jars,

a little fruit wine, incense like
a talisman. Half of these we took

as gifts to the infirmary,
leaving the rest for when the time came

to close the accounts, sell the house
with its furnishings complete. Those

who moved in afterwards, we found,
had all the right convictions.

HO 213/926
'Compulsory Repatriation of Undesirable Chinese Seamen, 1945–46'

Other times it's easy to turn out the light
on the top step, and as it goes,
see the shoes out of reach from the swing
and rattle of the door, so undisturbed,

yours like sentinels among the children's.
A late bus takes the corner, locked in speed,
its long growl rising from the kerb to lift
it from itself, *all sound*, as if at this hour

it is nothing else but an order of things –
with a common enough purpose –
that takes place, and throws its dead weight
on the road dockside now becoming visible.

*

If I'd gotten up they would've knocked me down.
If I'd spoken up there would've been hell to pay.
If I'd brought it up again I'd have lost my job.
If I'd taken it up they wouldn't let me stay.

If I'd messed it up my wife would've kicked me out.
If I'd played it up my friends would've had a go.
If I'd given it up who would've told you so?
If I'd made it up trust me you'd never know.

*

Twice now, she says, he's woken in pain.
Nothing will calm him. In the morning
they'll find a night ferry gone aground
near Wallasey, not an hour before the boy
cried out, and it'll make her wonder. Sometimes
she has the same dream she thinks he's had,
watchmen waking to the deadly dance of ships,
trapped in their own tonnage, an unnamed sea –

sometimes it's only a storm, which is kinder,
though the sound, when it happens, is the same.
It takes all I've got to remind her she's *not
alone, he was our friend too, nobody knows
what happened.* The boy's seven,
and my daughter goes to school with him.

*

Past closing at the Stevedore. *We knock
back the years, talk gear and children,*

*plans for the house now that war is over.
Next thing, light cracks across the floor*

*and as the door flings wide Jim can't
stop them, though I've seen him take*

*a body and throw it overboard. They're looking
for a man, this height, this face, anyone?*

*The crowd parts, no questions. Then they're on
the street again, marching our man along*

with his head down, sorry for the trouble,
if you'll just come with us and no fuss now.

Slowly we turn back to our drink.
In the near dark it could have been anyone.

*

Light fog on the harbour, and the new ships
gliding sweetly into place. Once, we lived
for the peal that told us we'd come to dock,

the hull still ringing for hours underfoot
after finding its berth. These days the warehouse
is an art museum, and the children tell me

when there's a show in town. I'd go if I could,
though there's no way to know if he won't
be there too, spinning a fine yarn, or holding

a glass to his ear – some trick he used to do –
all the better, he'd say, if you weren't listening,
all the better to hear the sea coming in.

CAMERATA

We left the back room of the palace locked
where the king, hearing of the fleet's approach,

had stood quickly from his untouched meal
to find his son against the sky's black sail.

Something about that room, we later felt,
foretold catastrophe. Perhaps it was what

the servant said, hours before, who found
it swept by a hand not unlike her own,

the furniture – as if by a ghost – arranged
behind fastened doors. Or what it meant

to come upon the tall, paired mirrors thrown
from their frames in fright, hiding their brazen

infinities. A cup with its cracked lip
stood on the dresser, next to where he kept

close tally for each month the boy was gone.
We could still see his numbers in the stone,

like a child's, their straight lines not touching,
endings rubbed out where they were too long.

The last ones extended right to the floor.
And that is why we had to lock the doors.

THE CRABS
Langkawi, December 2004

All afternoon we followed as they fled
across the sand, scooping them unawares
in our soft palms to where the older boys
worked on the defences: heights and towers
around a cliff-edged pit. Here we dropped
our struggling prey, stopping only to laugh
at how the more we caught, the harder
they threw themselves against the banks,
as if they also found in not being few
some greater urgency of escape.

Two weeks later, when the world unlatched
we heard in cadences that we could name
grief like a wall of water, the sea coming in
after dark to fill our shallow moat,
break all the windows, and with skint hands
lift our captives up as if from one death
wide-eyed, limbs flung into another.

THE WAY LIGHT WORKS[*]

they'll say it isn't good for you but if you paid attention

for about an hour each morning you could look at the sun

when it puts its head up it's still the colour of cheap vests

keep looking & it turns white   an O   like a speed-sign

or the moon when they show it in pictures   I learn that

the way light works this happens to everything   I can see

through my fingers   dropped leaves pretend they're alive

the bus-stop is full of tiles that are orange as persimmons

when those are cut into little squares they won't even stay

on your tongue   why call these safety vests I think they

just make us seem dangerous   I was standing at the bus-

stop   with Vinoth   who would be turning twenty-four

except the bus didn't   why call it a speed-sign   in the

After a traffic accident in late 2017 in which twenty-five migrant labourers were killed in Tuas, Singapore.

evening they call & say before six it's hard to see anything

when boss answers he looks the other way so we can't see his

lips   no matter   for now all I have are these questions &

not just about the things we call things   how come they say

morning has broken   I am still a citizen of the morning

FIRST EASTER

'This shall be unto you the beginning of months,
the first month of the year unto you…'
— Exodus 12:2

Days pass, without miracle. I learn the shapes
sunlight makes as it spills from her fingers, bends
with ease, a thread of gold playing at her ankles.

Against the window she is frail as cotton, folds
like a song into the cushion-covers. *Why have you*
come, she asks? Each time I try a different answer:

to leave the other place, to have plenty, to start
over. She laughs her silent laughter – all breath – so
the room trembles with her, tells what she remembers

of leaving her firstborn with the neighbours,
knotting jade bracelets into a sleeve, going
to clean houses. Months, barely, younger

than I am. *And everything was precious then,*
she laughs again, *now our bread falls straight*
from the heavens! I rearrange the pillows, listen

as evening rises and falls around her, darkens
her hair, lets a country of shadows settle on her
shoulders. *This is more than plenty,* I want to say,

even if someone has turned the river downstairs
into stone. *More than we can hold.* Her eyes are
somewhere else, unseeing, but they already kno

LUCKY

for Arlyn Nucos and Abigail Leste*

Fortune enters by an open door. Unlatched,
a window brings a double blessing, as joy leftover
spills surely into a neighbour's soil. Debts
unpaid at midnight will always last the year,

while pockets, filled with coins, will never empty
unless leaving from one threshold to another, one
neglects to take a gift: the curse of plenty.
When choosing a new abode, it should be seen

that the stairs fall in pairs (not in threes), the better
to avoid that third unlucky element
that comes with 'gold' and 'silver'. What follows after
must not be named; no, not ever written –

even on this last Lord's day of the going year
as another decade shuffles at the gate
still far from home, and already getting older.
No envelope was made to hold its weight.

mestic workers killed in a traffic accident outside Lucky Plaza, Singapore.

MY LOVE,

What's mine is yours: 1. a floor swept clean
and lifted to the sky, the work of my hands,

all its inches free of the earth that billows
through the open windows. 2. Windows, scoured

with cloth and then newspaper (so the fibres
don't stick), 3. the book, ring-bound, where I've stuck

our news from home. 4. A home, yes, and one full
of children whose hands are now familiar

to my touch, their paths to school a map of everything
I know, each with her small truths

and misdemeanours *[N.B. among the lies I've come
to count as debt, these are without doubt*

the most precious.] 5. Nothing precious, 6. with which
to make a show of love, 7. to give (and even

if it's better) to receive. […] 8. Room enough
for one, 9. a shadow, 10. a stack of folded things,

11. a sound. 12. All the light that's within reach
and 13. falls without accident, and 14. is found.

** 'I know I shouldn't bother in her personal affair but when she is using our
home phone to chit chat with her lover…it bothers me!!' – 'How To Deal With
Maid With Boyfriend??', kiasuparents.com*

GUNUNG[*]

1965

My love has built a house among the mountains,
the mountains are a shadow for my love.

He has named every tree upon the mountain,
no mountain is a mountain for my love.

Who has seen his shadow on the mountains?
The women in the village speak of my love

in low voices, they tell me that their husbands
have glimpsed the erring shadow of my love.

In truth they know no more than the mountains.
Ask them, you will learn nothing of my love.

They say that he who lives among the mountains
must sleep without the shadow of his love

but my shadow falls across our hidden places
and a mountain sleeps within the house of love.

One day he will leave the shadowed mountains.
One day he will build our common house.

Till then my love will sleep among the mountains.
A far and trembling mountain is my love.

2015

This will be my eighth year in this country.
Three years in my first house, four in this one

where I am treated well, sometimes like a nurse
for their two children, sometimes also

like a daughter. My own are still at school,
and as my husband, who works long hours

in Bandung tells me, are happy there, each
content with her sister for company

and obedient, or at least keeps to herself.
I call home less these days than in those first

exacting years, find equal joy in walking up
the slope to where the girls wait for their bus,

a hill which (I've learnt) till now remembers
a boy who drove branches thick as his arms

into the earth to save his village, but could not save
himself from a king who knew nothing

of love but as a threat, and so was killed. Here
he comes, the mountain breathes his name.

*gunung: Bahasa Indonesia word for 'mountain'.

OPERATION THUNDERSTORM

Codename for the Singapore Armed Forces' operation to intercept, detain or deter all refugees fleeing South Vietnam after the fall of Saigon in 1975.

As if we were not once also torrential,
unstoppable and overboard, our bodies
following our hands across the swell
to this fistful of soil, not so much to build
as to stay afloat, fingers closing round
its buttress roots, stern breakwater,
an island peopled only by our leaving?

All through the years, we fell as rain
and though there was little to catch us then
gathered in every small indentation,
by always seeking out the softest earth
made each channel fit for a monsoon,
with time made the rivers and reservoirs,
made our children *drink and not forget the source* –

except it is never a river's source
that then undoes it, that moves the land
to its throat to stop it singing, or stands
a bridge upon its straits to wedge the banks
apart, digs clean through its bed to put
the currents underground; so the storms,
abundant, must send their ships elsewhere

to drop anchor beyond the locked heart
of the bay, while the sea herself, come knocking,
finds no harbour, and though our own cross
over the dredged marsh as on dry sand
without danger, or really knowing why,
their thirst seems to come straight from the water,
every fresh glass an exile from the sky.

WAYS OF WALKING

*After a series of paintings by Alvin Ong: for the pilgrims of Santiago
and the refugees of Oxford, UK*

i.
(Finisterre)

In the place you have come to know as home
you see the shapes of your friends, sleeping
by the embers, and the fragile light
of a day's small achievements burning gently.
One evening at the fire he tells you, come!
there is more beyond the red line of the shore.
you walk across the lake which is the night,
and the boat, taking your weight, begins to move.

ii.
(We Will Meet Again)

This is the road: at times a gathering
for the ones you leave, and those you meet
on the same margins, who leave you trembling.
Other times it is the mystery
at the water's edge, where a shifting line
of salt skitters up and down the sand
leaving, in places, the fragments of a ship,
a cask of coins, light brimming on the stones.

iii.
(Past Life)

There is nothing to fear about these trees
or the shadows they make – the width of the path,
a cloth for the creatures of the night.
This is the truth you have been taught. And yet
so distant the stranger with the golden staff
setting the air ablaze, that for days you wait
in a dark hollow, unsure of yourself
and the strength of your lamp, before setting off.

iv.
(Into Great Silence)

How the road stands before you like a room
between here – which you cannot see – and there,
which approaches the colour of basalt
but is only a reflection of things
you must go outside these walls to look at!
See how this sun, which is like the sun, except
from a film or a dream, returns your stare?
See the figure on your left, departing?

v.
(We Longed for the Night)

In this scene there are no travellers
or followers, no inns or guest-houses,
no forest and no undergrowth, no hot
hard earth the colour of indecision.
In a field of wheat the unseen river
draws the village dogs into its shade
and you, rubbing your eyes at the sight,
not slowing down, not daring to believe.

vi.
(The Visitation)

As between day and night there is a bridge
of many colours separating
what is seen in trees and the branches of trees
and what is heard, flowing to the sea, you meet
one who has no stick or cloak, but walks
surely in your direction. He begins
to tell you everything he has seen, which is
a story of all the stories you have heard.

vii.
(The Miracle)

It happens like this: the unknown crowd
filling the square, clamouring to see
the man of many miracles, and you,
you who have walked for days without stopping,
praying that the unexpected rain
would not stand between you and this meeting,
closing your fingers on his trodden hem.
Not a word. A healing takes hold of you.

viii.
(The Wanderer's Nightsong)

After the waking, the walking, the day's
easy joy, the road does not end. You arrive
at a bank where others are also waiting
for the voice of a boatman, like a wind
dwelling gently over the water.
What can it be like to know when thunder
comes, but not rain? On the surface
there is clear light, movement, a rising chain.

ix.
(A Shadow and a Dream)

Young traveller, when the road becomes narrow
see the ones returning and take heart.
There they are, standing in their clothes of gold.
Their ways are your ways, their manners and tongues
your own, even their eyes which are your eyes
are not a day older. Not far now.
This is the road that swims between two seas.
This is the earth that lifts into the light.

MARGINALIA

101 Special Training School, where 165 Malayan
Communists (later the Malayan People's Anti-Japanese Army)
were trained by the British ahead of the Japanese Occupation.

i. *This is the façade of a two-storey building...*

someone has smuggled joss onto the grounds
a smell of worship   through the window-slats
covers the desks   the knife-bitten desks
cabinet   chairs   *all that in them is*

they search our possessions   such thin papers
bearing nothing   but the names of our gods
are hard to find   recalcitrant
they cloud the earth   set the air alight

..., home of an Armenian billionaire, located

ii. *at Tanjong Balai near the mouth of Jurong...*

seven thirty p.m.   that which is silent is silent
we kneel by the path outside the house
wipe every broken part   pass a thread
through the barrel   till it comes out white

in the thick dusk it must seem   as if
we are panning for gold   our hands dipped
with grease   all the pieces   immaculate
the dry ground a stream   of precious metal

...River. It was a large ornamental bungalow

III. *with Chinese style pavilions. [Used] to train...*

we exercise before dawn   sometimes
in the dead hours   drills that will ready us
for what must be   soon a kind   of not-being
intent   and yet without sight   or trace

lithe even   in other words unknowable
the wind picking up its feet   a cracking
of shells on the beach   under sand
fishermen   walking over last night's hatch

...soldiers for anti-Japanese guerrilla work

IV. *in Malaya. The site was later taken over...*

we are being prepared   for eventualities
to hold down   the rhythm of wanting
give ourselves apace   to what comes
who we will be   cannot know   this

also a kind of being   this strange alliance
this   putting to sleep   making new
by native men under European instructions[1]
still a surfeit   yes   a dreaming   of a kind

...by the Government during the development

v. of Jurong Industrial Estate in the 1960s.

soon   the month of ghosts   a month also
of songs   all the best places   set aside
a full harvest   on empty thresholds
surely now the old ways will abandon us

let the sealed earth   remain now let its rafters
hold   let the children play   among the graves
let them   know what this means   let us
too   make of this   letting   a letting go

Copyright. Title devised by Library staff. [2]

[1] *From a report by Sumida Haruzo, officer of the Japanese Kempeitai
in occupied Singapore*
[2] *From archival notes in the Print Heritage collection, National
Library Board, Singapore*

SOPHIA

In 1818, Sir Thomas Stamford Raffles, newlywed husband of Sophia,
Governor-General of Bencoolen, surveyed the island of Singapore,
which was made a British colony in early 1819.

I.
12 December, 1818.
Governor-General's Residence, Bencoolen.

Last night, my love, I took the nameless book
that arrived with our mail on Thursday's ship
and sat down to read. In that shapely dark
one by one the servants kept their hours,
leaving the gate unlocked (as you prefer)
as they crept downhill to their inventions.
Nothing moved, but on the forest's lip
something glimmered with a sailor's patience:

a slip of light, a turning in the shallows,
an unmade sea scuffing the glass surface
with its swallowed things. I thought of you,
the men in their tossing berths, the night's
empty heat, and beyond the shoal of islands
a breath of earth, void, then the firmament.

12 December, 1858.
Highwood House, Mill Hill, London.

This remains sharpest in my memory:
the day you went walking into the wind
from a corner of that special island
so spectral now, yet with its harbour, then
the pearl of our possessions. How we made
our livings there, rejoicing as we found
a world so large, and of our own devising,
that you longed to know it, end to end.

As the light fell short you came back trembling,
stood bareheaded in the dowsing rain, yelled
for a mirror. Told how even the men
had fled when they saw you approaching, pale
arms outstretched in a token of friendship.
I held on to your hands and let you weep.

THE DIFFERENCE

'They came crowding to see what the Franks looked like, and they
were all astonished and said, "These are white Bengalis!" Around each
Frank was a crowd of Malays: some twisting his beard, some taking off
his hat, some grasping his hand…'
    — Sejarah Melayu, Ch. 29.

This is how we knew the difference: eyes
like porcelain. Cheeks that flushed at sea
from thirst and stale wine, arms white as snow
soft to the touch, a shout beneath our hands.
The way they stood, without ceremony,
thighs aching from the long walk up the sand,
their shoes. Their hardened faces, sharp as prows.
When they came in the middle of a dry

season we knew they meant no good or ill,
carried nothing. Out of the empty hull
they gave themselves into our company,
worshipped at our tables, sat down to eat
from the same dishes. When the month was up
we walked across the water to their ships
with bread and writhing fish for a long journey…
In the end, our children will ask, what was it

that gave them away at the next monsoon?
Instead of skin, steel. Instead of matted
curls swept back with laughter, casques. Instead
of sails emblazoned with the afternoon's
sun, these shadows on the harbour: turrets
laced with pikes, burning fat, the smell
of anchovies, saltpetre. When we fell
at a distance, it was as if we'd never met.

TRANSFORMATIONS
or, six translations of Meng Haoran's 'Spring Dawn'

for Hong Kong

春曉

春眠不覺曉，
處處聞啼鳥。
夜來風雨聲，
花落知多少。
　　— 孟浩然

o.

The seasons have changed with a sudden force
and the birds, who know, cannot keep the peace.

1.

The peace, we know, is a bitter thing.
It has been washed in the eye of the harbour.

Those who live here have tasted of it.
Their tongues betray the loss of a harbour.

A use of force can be read as betrayal.
It is full of the heat of the harbour.

We must hold our own, others say.
They are held in the stone of the harbour.

The windows are carved high in the walls.
What comes through is the smell of the harbour.

Our children look up, and see a light.
They have not tired of dawn in the harbour.

All they know are what's fallen in the streets.
These were the flowers of fragrant harbour.

2 .

But no, nothing here like a whiff of flowers.
Only the port's salt odour, a pungent faith
scorching wet canvas as the wind turns south
and something else arrives across the water –

a troubling heat, bearing the sweetest haze,
with all we know of worship and of pain
lifted up to heaven in that man-made scent.
A boy, soundless, shoulders the excess

of *agar* and sandalwood, nearly a month's
shipment, hauls the sacks to the jetty's edge
while out at sea our husbands become gods
whose lives are also in the storm's own hands.

3.

No-one hears the birds
beating the air into song.
This is the first sleep.

No-one keeps a count
as Spring is cut from the trees.
This is the second.

4.

Night carries on, though here also are those
for whom each morning is a stolen thing.
Without the city's stale heat they wake,
lift themselves with wan arms and come to us,
who are still sleeping, in our crescent light.
All is in their hands. It is they who make
new in our absence what is seen, unseen.
Their shining faces put the birds to flight.

(Only they know what happens in the dark:
a harbour buried whole, leaving nothing
but the tallest lights – red – above the storm
while the island hunkers deep within its ark.
Seeing this, they carry us from dawn to dawn.
Rising, we banish them from room to room.)

5.

a storm   is a song   a ship sings
    when wide   above   the high waters
sleep falls   like a cloud   no sound

    the wives   do not weep   at the shore
the watchmen   do not cry   for land
    even birds   are felled   in flight

their wings   filling up   with gale
    their feet   crossed   for a dive
but nothing comes   the air   is still

    the face   of the deep   does not move
all we see   are the feet   lost in iron
    all we hear   are the hollows   of the sea

GRAVITY

'A team of physicists announced on Thursday that they had heard and recorded the sound of two black holes colliding, a fleeting chirp that fulfilled the last prophecy of Einstein's theory.'
— *New York Times*, 11 February 2016

In the firefighter's dawn, a waking jolt
shook a scientist's needle in its bracket.

Our storm-flensed heaven made no sign of rain.
We went about our business, unaware

of what would come of that discovery
while somewhere unnoticed, a faithful eye

tracked our orbit: an errant planet caught
mid-push and pull, the struggle out of sight

from us, who were its blest inhabitants.
Quietly, we left the ageless distance

to our best instruments. But this morning
was different. I heard it too, the song

from out beyond the rim of all we were
where one absence languished for another.

EVA

After you had gone to bed, that night,
a wind came and touched a corner of the roof
which sang, through the shingles that had come loose
and shook the nest, which had been built inside.
How late, the storm that followed close behind
locked in all its pent determination
that even love's sentry was, briefly, then,
asleep, her once watchful head dipped within,

so made no sound as, like a ship astern,
her bower was rushed by the northern rain.
This morning I saw her young: unlearned,
alive. I cannot explain, love, but I knew
how different they seemed, and how they sang
all the louder in the rain, and flew.

LOCH NA FUAICHE
from Cong, 25 minutes via R345 and R300.

No telling on this drive, what must
take years to know: how love is found

in a valley delta, where two fields meet
in stone – a low wall, raised here by hand

from the slow gathering on either side
of rock, large enough to unearth a crop

or throw a plough sideways. A difficult task
given how, from near the mountaintop

each spring, loosed in its thaw,
the river brings new boulders toward the sea

and leaves them by the weir. Or even how
faintly the loch wears the county's edge

till fields are sunk, and disappear
with a season's planting, all their names

and boundaries intact. Every now and then
a winter still comes to fill the glen

so all we can see is the black backbone
of our stones underwater, no more a wall

but a path, flood-lit in the shallow depths,
that links the far sides of the loch, and then

rises, to join hands with the lifting land.

NOTES ON A LANDSCAPE

'The mountainous landscape, wide-open spaces, harsh climate and long
winter darkness have made it easy to imagine ghosts, trolls and other
supernatural creatures lurking around every corner.'
— A Traveller's Guide to Icelandic Folk Tales

i. Reynisdrangar | Rock

In one version a pair of giants
have taken a man's wife. There he stands
protesting, two jagged arms raised
like pillars, till the water takes his voice.
In another, somewhat lesser known,
the giants are hauling a ship, stolen
from its fleet in a terrible storm,
to shore when daylight steals over them.

See how the earth leaps to remember us?
Though the giants' faces have gone, unnoticed,
other features are still clear –
sailors stiff with shock, and the old farmer
who knows his life is of no consequence
but gives it anyway, before your eyes.

ii. Skóga | River

You can see the tides that take their names
brawling in the river. Here is Thrasi,
son of Thorolf, a traveller, whose fame
must be chanced at sea; there is
Lodmundur, wonder-worker, who pines
after land. Every man's heart is fashioned
between these banks. Half will remain
on a path to the ocean, half will long

for an icy shore. Late in life, we are told,
Thrasi hides his chest of worldly treasures
behind a waterfall, and many arrive
to seek their wealth. No-one says: where
snow covers the crater, there is silver.
Where the bees have their fill, there is gold.

iii. Goðafoss | Waterfall

After Thorgeir has made up his mind
he goes home, gathers up the gods
dozing by the fire, carries them –
still sleeping – to the water's edge. It takes
an hour to row to where the gully's
darkest, and as he hefts them overboard
it's not the cold solemn plunge
that wakes them, not even the words

Thorgeir repeats to keep ill luck at bay,
but the gasp of the stream as it takes
their unworldly weight, a caving
in the wall, the earth's dark heave going under.
Next morning we see the empty hillside,
nearly slip on the dead fish in the gate.

iv. Náttfaravík | Cove

Remember the one about brave Náttfari
who cast away in a stolen rowboat,
taking to sea with his family
and all of Gardar's best horses on board?
The books will tell you how he came ashore
in a quiet cove, no more a slave
but a man of his own name, a settler,
saved by foresight and his will to live.

Remember this instead: how one night
after they have fought, again, his wife steps
out on the pier to find the chains untied,
the oarsmen on their legendary way.
How when they grow old she'll laugh herself to bed
as he tells us how wise he was, and brave.

v. Berserkjagata | Way

Styr has had enough of the two madmen,
their voices careening over the earth
like carts fastened to broken stallions.
The afternoon he finds one of them
asleep by the well, a pale bow
from a familiar throw
knotted in the boy's unclasping hand,
Styr gives them shirts he has cut from a bear,

sets them to clearing a path through the plain
between his father's farmstead and the sea.
All day they bring the crumpled stone
into the yard, until Styr pushes the wall
over where they lie sleeping. No-one knows
if this tale is told true, or tall.

vi. Viðgelmir | Cave

Under the earth's long burn, a hearth.
Under the bright expanse, kindling.
tefan hauls his sack of dripping heather
under the valley's lip, hangs his damp things
from cracks in the rock. Nearly a month
since the whispered meetings, their careful
plans wrecked by that idiot Ingolfsson
who should never have been given a role

anyway. Now Stefan moves in the dead
of the night, and only as far
as the lava's edge. From dreams of the crown –
to this! Our daughters warn their children
about the troll who lives in the caves,
whose song you'll hear if you go too near.

vii. Þórisdalur | *Valley*

Nothing[1] here reminds you of him.
His face does not set in the softest stone.
His feet, having fled, leave no prints.
The peaks do not resemble the turn
of his spine, pebbles look nothing
like his eyes. If you see in the distance
the too-tall shadow of a tree, he is
not there. There is nothing you can find.

----

[1] Only the sagas record that after
being outlawed, Grettir takes to these slopes,
stealing sheep to banish his hunger.
It's not likely that the stories are believed,
though those who repeat them can hope
otherwise. How else will they live?

WHAT FOLLOWS
Deer cull, Wytham

A moment's pause before a fist of swallows
spooks the sky above the nearest trees.
Something shakes the fence-bound rows,
bursts through bracken, reappears

on fallow earth: two deer, mud-sprayed
and plunged with melt, lips puckering
to a hoarsened bark, dark eyes like slate
fired in the run. My finger

leaves the shutter for long enough
that bounding across seed-rows they are gone,
the cracked frost making an ashen path
to a gap in the horse-wire thorn,

the next field, and the one beyond
where white tails vanish into wheat.
I look more closely at the ground.
Here they stood, and saw, and blinked back death

then turned with gunshot simplicity,
fled, like any creature would,
but struck on the flint of that eternity
more alive than in the burnished wood.

ROAD CUTTING AT GLANMIRE
'Gleann Maghair': the valley of ploughed land

They learned the hard way to a city's heart
was to drive a road into the mountain
like a river, lost between its own dry banks

with gravelled walls holding the earth in place
and fast-growing trees, for the wet topsoil.
A bypass. When it was finished they came

to see the cut that had been named after them,
mounting the ridge above its strange traffic
while their own valley of ploughed land rose

a stone's throw behind the black backbone
of the new highway. Far as I could tell
from the bus's window, these days the village

has a changed air, full of primary schools
and real estate. We passed a lovely church
near the auctioneer's, but without stopping

went on into Cork, taking the road which,
we were told, had been built at great cost
to shorten the journey into the city.

PULSE

after Wang Gungwu

I.

Take this, the city's wrist. Blood thunders
close to the surface, a curious blue
where the washed river's lost its bolder hues.
Or this, soft hollow of its temple,
where brushing past the first greying hairs one finds
an ardent throb young enough to send
a shiver down the spine. The method's simple:
it matters where you press your fingers –

no-one approaches the heart straight-on
(where currents mix) unless a life's at stake.
And at the thigh or even the crook
of the arm even the best physicians
might seek a vein in vain. Young scholar, be warned:
a pulse is not a voice, nor a voice a song.

II.

But what of these charts, these measurements
of growth, these predictions and prognoses?
Once premature, she's tallest in her class
by far, and now runs the quickest mile.
(Some say it was in her stars at birth; taught well,
a child can learn to prove even the most
unlikely fate.) We scour these numbers
for the luckiest traits, pray for portents

of what might come of her when we are old
and short of breath, and sight. Not what we know,
or think we know, nor what we're told -
though we will not hear when others tell us so.
It's hard enough to read the heart's direction.
What's buried here is more than circulation.

THE QUESTIONING

For Shrey Bhargava, questioned by the police after he made allegations of racial discrimination during the casting audition for a film.

I.

An actor is questioned by the police

And he tells them about the way pigment
arrives on the page, how in the old days
there was no accounting for how many
died at sea to bring Vermeer his blues,
or how the heaviest elements in van Gogh's
chrome would turn the man delirious,
though its poison could still not rival green's,
which left arsenic on Victorian fingers.

Even black – 'bone-black' – was once derived
from burning ivory, all through the years
of empire, an elephant in every room.
*But this on the screen, officer? This is
colourless!* A word his and not-his,
whose provenances are older than this.

II.

The police have questions for the actor

No, not a word from a script either,
although the script, in this case, is everything.

See how the first letter folds at the waist,
a body thrown backwards from a chair
while the second worries itself, a tail

with no legs to shelter between, the third –
curved like a moon or mollusc, is cryptic,
unknowable, like a child asleep –

III.

Questions are asked by the police

Of course it's not about how it looks.
It's what we hear, that single sorting syllable
made, tellingly perhaps, to rhyme with 'face'
though even that is negotiable: *did you think
we mean the same in every language*, as in,
that *our meanness is the same?* The way
these people have said it, you can't separate
the colour from thickness of skin. Throw in
weight too, for some are heavier at birth
though even now we have no measure of how
much a body will bear. *Don't you get it,
officer?* As in: *doesn't it get to you?*

IV.

The police ask if the actor has any questions

V.

The actor answers

It's hard to say, officer. When I came in
I had none, but now you've made me think.
Is there a word that is more than sound?
How do I pronounce what you've written down?

All I want is this. Tell me there's room
for all of what we cannot love, and whom.

LOVE POEM

'*Every poem is a love poem.*'
— Helen Mort

The truth comes to us late one afternoon:
a poem must love the thing it lives within.
The more we use the word, the more it means –

a poem must hold the thing, but tenderly,
not afraid, not holding off, and not too soon –
this truth comes to us late one afternoon

as we're sipping tea, and talking about poems,
or about love, the language they're written in.
The more we use that word, the more it seems

(no matter if we can know what we mean)
because the thing within is far more than
any truth that might come on an afternoon

and if a poem must live within that thing
then it must love the whims and edges of the thing,
beyond even what those words could mean.

Out there are all the things we want to mean
but do not say because we cannot know
what truths might come to us one afternoon

when talking about tea, or sipping love,
or writing poems even, using words
that mean more than all the things they mean.

So take this word that holds itself like a tune.
It's more than what will be and what has been.
The truth comes to us late one afternoon.
The more we use the word the more it means.

FIFTY-ONE

National Day, 2016

This year, it falls in the seventh month,
which is when the dead remember us.
Now that I live alone, I'll spend the morning
tending the fire in the urn downstairs:
the grass is red and white with last night's joss.

In the afternoon, if it doesn't rain,
I'll do the laundry. Take the curtains down,
hang out the sheets. It's hard to find
another day like this for a thorough clean.
Believe me. Something's always left undone.

Evenings are usually when I phone the girls.
Not today. It's a long weekend, so they'll have gone.
I'll take a walk instead, then lock the door.
It's said that most can't quite get past the step,
but you never know what spirits lurk beyond.

Mother used to say as we get older,
we take after our children more and more.
I'm not so sure. My second one is braver,
asks, every year, why I would bother.
My first won't even come close to our altar –

she's found something better to explain
what we're for, where we go to when we go.
Where else but here? That's what I'd like to know.
It was I who taught her to ask such questions.
With age, these are the things that start to show.

NOCTURNAL
for Grandmother

Look. This is the garden you have watered.
    In the wet season the grass grows over.
        Untrimmed, the hedge is still in flower.

We have set tables across your porch.
    Stacked them with plenty, more than we can ask.
        Above us, lights fill a second sky;

windows, left wide, sing the evening rain. Do
    you see? Over your shoulder an earthen bowl
        brims with ash and laughter, as guests come

to sit with us awhile. Their children and yours
    are playing at the swing. Their gifts are tucked
        among our twos and threes. Look

again. Late December, and the tree is hung
    with fruit. These are our faces, that are turning
        to salt. Our feet that linger and are now stone.

FINAL CUT
Walter's, Oxford

Four days to leaving, he has his hair done,
lets her cradle his head, turn it from side
to side. Behind each ear the slow blade
moves, removes strands that have taken root
of their own accord: tenacious, out of sight,
secure in knowledge of their chosen plot.

The pressure is just right. So for a while,
feet angled over the floor, he travels
all alone in that uncertain room framed
by the chair, lights. Finding the mirror
too close, he closes his eyes, approximates
the thirteen-hour night between *to* and *from,*

sun warming the earth enough in sleep
to set him on his way. Among the things
he'll never fathom, this conspiracy of air –
how a cold morning, or unexpected rain
(so often making one city feel like another)
might, given perfect conditions, transform

into a river high above the rough surface
of this sea-level, waiting to lift or leave us.
On cue, a draught enters the shop, sends
his cut ends into heavy drifts, banks. No-one
watches, but he wonders if it is like a dance.
Which are coming, which the leaving ones.

MOVING HOUSE

These are things that shake us in our sleep:
doors left open, drawers, the bare-backed chair
that still, without a coat, swivels gently,
books in boxes. Pictures taken down, squares
of darker paint turned over to the sun,
and above all, their wiring undone,
the lights' glass tubes put away in plastic.

Once is enough. The eye learns to plot
all of this in each new habitation,
recognize the empty room's joints, pivots,
dimensions – every house has a skeleton –
while the body learns it must carry less
from place to place, a kind of tidiness
that builds, hardens. Some call it fear,

of change, or losing what we cannot keep.
Others, experience. Truth is, it has no name
or station, and only the weight we give.
Old friend, I feel its steep tug again
this evening, across wire and lens
as you show me the house, a bare continent.
(These are things that shake us in our sleep.)

ACKNOWLEDGEMENTS

The author is grateful to the editors of the following publications, where several of these poems were previously featured: *Adroit, Ambit, Antiphon, Berfrois, Cha, The Compass, Eastlit, Honest Ulsterman, Hunger Mountain, Hyphen, The Interpreter's House, The Irish Examiner, The Learned Pig, The London Magazine, Mekong Review, The Missing Slate, Oxford Review of Books, Oxonian Review, POEM, PN Review, Quarterly Literary Review Singapore,* and *Wildness.*

'Monologue for *Noh* Masks' was commissioned by the Pitt Rivers Museum, Oxford, while 'gunung' and 'My Love' were commissioned by Poetry Festival Singapore. Some of the poems have also appeared in chapbooks or anthologies by Chameleon Press, Hong Kong; Landmark Books and Math Paper Press, Singapore; as well as Carcanet Press and Smith | Doorstop, UK.